Tick Tock

Written by Mollie Schofield
Illustrated by Alessandro Valdrighi

Collins

Tag sits on the mat.

It *is* Nic!

Nic and Tag sit on the mat.

tick tock
tick tock

tap tap tap

tap tap tap

Dot and Kit!

Tick tock

🐾 Review: After reading 🐾

Use your assessment from hearing the children read to choose any GPCs, words or tricky words that need additional practice.

Read 1: Decoding

- Turn to page 5 and point to **tick tock**. Ask: Is this a sound or a name? How do you know? (e.g. *it's a sound because Tag is wondering who/what it is*)
- Ask the children to read the following and to point to the pairs of letters that make one sound. (/c/ "ck")

  mat   tock   tick   tap   Dot   is

- Point to the characters' names on pages 7 and 10. Say: Can you blend in your head when you read these names?

Read 2: Prosody

- Model reading page 4, then on page 5, point to **tick tock** and ask: How should I say these words?
- Encourage the children to read **tick tock** at different speeds and in different tones. Ask: What sounds best? Why?
- Draw the children's attention to the exclamation marks on pages 6 and 10. Explain that this punctuation tells the reader that this sentence should be read with feeling. Model reading the two sentences using your voice to show surprise or relief or that something is funny.

Read 3: Comprehension

- Ask the children if they have heard mysterious noises that turned out to be something ordinary.
- Say to the children: If you were telling a friend about this book, would you describe it as a horror story, a funny story or a mystery story? Why? (e.g. *a mystery story because there are mysterious sounds*)
- Ask the children to retell the story using the pictures on pages 14 and 15. Can they tell the story in the correct sequence and name the characters? Ask:
  - Who is asking the question at the beginning? (*Tag*) What can he hear? (*a tick tock sound and a tap sound*)
  - How does the story end? (*Dot and Kit come in and Tag finds out they were making some of the sounds*)
- Bonus content: Ask the children to make up a new story about a mysterious sound. They can use pages 2 and 3, deciding who hears the noise first, where it is coming from, and who/what it turns out to be as Tag explores the rooms.